# Kwanzaa

## by Lola M. Schaefer

Consulting Editor: Gail Saunders-Smith, Ph.D.

Consultant: Christine Patterson
Professor of African American History
Indiana University–Purdue University
Fort Wayne, Indiana

## Pebble Books

an imprint of Capstone Press
Mankato, Minnesota

Pebble Books are published by Capstone Press,
151 Good Counsel Drive, P.O. Box 669, Mankato, Minnesota 56002.
www.capstonepress.com

Printed in the United States of America, North Mankato, Minnesota.
072011   006231CGVMI

*Library of Congress Cataloging-in-Publication Data*
Schaefer, Lola M., 1950–
   Kwanzaa / by Lola M. Schaefer.
   p. cm.—(Holidays and celebrations)
   Includes bibliographical references and index.
   Summary: Simple text and photographs describe and illustrate the holiday that
was created in 1966 to honor African Americans.
   ISBN-13: 978-0-7368-0663-3 (hardcover)
   ISBN-10: 0-7368-0663-6 (hardcover)
   ISBN-13: 978-0-7368-4901-2 (paperback)
   ISBN-10: 0-7368-4901-7 (paperback)
   1. Kwanzaa—Juvenile literature. 2. Afro-Americans—Juvenile literature. 3.
United States—Social life and customs—Juvenile literature. [1. Kwanzaa. 2. Holidays.
3. Afro-Americans.] I. Title. II. Series.
   GT4403 .S37  2001
   394.261—dc21                                              00-023055

## Note to Parents and Teachers

The Holidays and Celebrations series supports national social
studies standards related to culture. This book describes Kwanzaa
and illustrates how it is celebrated. The photographs support early
readers in understanding the text. The repetition of words and
phrases helps early readers learn new words. This book also
introduces early readers to subject-specific vocabulary words, which
are defined in the Words to Know section. Early readers may need
assistance to read some words and to use the Table of Contents,
Words to Know, Read More, Internet Sites, and Index/Word List
sections of the book.

# Table of Contents

4

Kwanzaa is a holiday that honors African American culture. Kwanzaa celebrates the history and unity of all African Americans.

African American leader
Maulana Karenga created
Kwanzaa in 1966. He
wanted to teach African
Americans about their
African history.

| December | | | | | | |
|---|---|---|---|---|---|---|
| S | M | T | W | T | F | S |
| | | | | | 1 | 2 |
| 3 | 4 | 5 | 6 | 7 | 8 | 9 |
| 10 | 11 | 12 | 13 | 14 | 15 | 16 |
| 17 | 18 | 19 | 20 | 21 | 22 | 23 |
| 24 | 25 | 26 | 27 | 28 | 29 | 30 |
| 31 | | | | | | |

| January | | | | | | |
|---|---|---|---|---|---|---|
| S | M | T | W | T | F | S |
| | 1 | 2 | 3 | 4 | 5 | 6 |
| 7 | 8 | 9 | 10 | 11 | 12 | 13 |
| 14 | 15 | 16 | 17 | 18 | 19 | 20 |
| 21 | 22 | 23 | 24 | 25 | 26 | 27 |
| 28 | 29 | 30 | 31 | | | |

African Americans celebrate Kwanzaa from December 26 through January 1. Kwanzaa is similar to harvest festivals in Africa.

## The Seven Symbols of Kwanzaa

crops
mat
candle holder
corn
seven candles
unity cup

African Americans use seven symbols for Kwanzaa. Each symbol has a special meaning.

## The Seven Principles of Kwanzaa

unity
self-determination
collective work and responsibility
cooperative economics
purpose
creativity
faith

One symbol is a set of seven candles. Each candle stands for one of the seven Kwanzaa principles.

African Americans light
a different candle each
day during Kwanzaa. They
talk about the meaning
of each principle.

African Americans celebrate with a Kwanzaa meal on December 31. Everyone brings food to share.

Families and friends celebrate with African music and dancing. Children open gifts.

Everyone shouts "Harambee" during Kwanzaa. Harambee means "let's all pull together."

**candle**—a stick of wax with a wick running through it; the seven candles of Kwanzaa represent the seven principles of Kwanzaa.

**celebrate**—to do something fun on a special day; African Americans celebrate Kwanzaa for seven days in December and January.

**honor**—to show respect or to praise; Kwanzaa honors African Americans and their culture.

**principle**—a basic truth or belief; the seven principles of Kwanzaa can serve as guides for daily living.

**symbol**—a design or an object that stands for something else; the seven symbols of Kwanzaa are crops, a mat, a candle holder, corn, seven candles, a unity cup, and gifts; two extra symbols for Kwanzaa are a flag and a poster of the seven principles.

**unity**—the state of being together as one; Kwanzaa is a time of unity for African Americans.

# Read More

**Ford, Juwanda G.** *K is for Kwanzaa: A Kwanzaa Alphabet Book.* New York: Scholastic, 1997.

**Grier, Ella.** *Seven Days of Kwanzaa: A Holiday Step Book.* New York: Viking, 1997.

**Jones, Amy Robin.** *Kwanzaa.* Chanhassen, Minn.: Child's World, 2000.

**Rau, Dana Meachen.** *Kwanzaa.* A True Book. New York: Children's Press, 2000.

# Internet Sites

FactHound offers a safe, fun way to find Internet sites related to this book.

Go to *www.facthound.com*

He'll fetch the best sites for you!

**FactHound will fetch the best sites for you!**

# Index/Word List

**Word Count: 143**
**Early-Intervention Level: 13**

**Editorial Credits**
Mari C. Schuh, editor; Heather Kindseth, designer; Kimberly Danger and
  Heidi Schoof, photo researchers

**Photo Credits**
AP/Wide World Photos, 6
David F. Clobes, 4, 8, 14, 16
Lawrence Migdale, 10
Mark Adams/FPG International LLC, cover
Philip Emeagwali, 1
Photo Network/Esbin-Anderson, 18 (bottom)
Susanne Thornburg, 20
Unicorn Stock Photos/Nancy Ferguson, 12; Aneal F. Vohra, 18 (top)

Special thanks to Keith Mayes, a research consultant and doctoral candidate at
Princeton University's history department, for reviewing this book.